# Bridge Pamphlet
## No. 9

Richard Scott was born in London in 1981. His poems have appeared widely in magazines including *Poetry Review*, *Poetry London* and *Butt Magazine*. He has been a winner of the Wasafiri New Writing Prize, a Jerwood/Arvon Poetry Mentee and a member of the Aldeburgh 8. He teaches poetry at the University of Hertfordshire and talks about opera and libretti on Resonance FM.

# Wound

RICHARD SCOTT

Dearest Ben,
you are great!
please keep writing
totally wonderful
songs
'love Richard x

**THE RIALTO**

## ACKNOWLEDGEMENTS

Many thanks to the editors of the following journals and anthologies, where several of these poems first appeared: *Poetry Review, The Rialto, Poetry London, Butt Magazine, Magma, The Poetry of Sex* and *Best British Poetry 2014.*

Heartfelt thanks to the following organisations which have supported my writing through mentorship, money, advice and care: The Arvon Foundation, The Poetry Trust, Aldeburgh Music, The Poetry Society, Goldsmiths College, Faber & Faber and Jerwood Charitable Foundation.

Love for the following people who helped shape this pamphlet with their advice and kindness: Daljit Nagra, Edward Doegar, Abigail Parry, Fiona Moore, Michael Mackmin, Chrissy Williams, Liz Berry, Rebecca Morrison, Hannah Lowe, Julia Reckless, Rhona Johnson, Mum, Dad, Hilary, Gerard and Daniel ♥ Theophanous.

## BRIDGE PAMPHLETS

This is the ninth in a series of *The Rialto* pamphlets designed to cross the gap between magazine and book publication for new writers or, for established writers, that between collections. Previous pamphlets have been by Lorraine Mariner, Richard Lambert, Peter Sansom, Hannah Lowe, Jen Campbell, Janet Rogerson, Luke Samuel Yates, Laura Scott, Emily Wills and Kate Wakeling.

The Publisher acknowledges financial assistance from Grants For Arts.

**LOTTERY FUNDED**

The Rialto is a Registered Charity No. 297553
Typeset in Berling 10 on 12.5pt. Design by Starfish, Norwich
Printed in England by Page Bros, Norwich, Norfolk
Cover illustration: Antonio Pollaiuolo - Battle of the Nudes (C1470).

*For Edward, Daljit and Daniel.*

# CONTENTS

Through you I drain the pent up rivers of myself

*Walt Whitman*


You say that this is all there is:
sweat and piss and blood and jizz.

*Michael Robbins*

# CHILDHOOD

*Can I come with you?* asked the clown
in his caterpillar-green silk jump-suit.

*If you're going to say no then give me a crisp!*
He spat, thrusting his fist spelt    L        O        V        E

into the open mouth of my Golden Wonder.
Crumbs stuck to his chapped lips.

I watched his grey beard struggle for freedom
under a smear of hastily applied pan-stick,

I counted the missing buttons on his coat,
the soup-stains on his ruff . . .

*Can I come with you or not, you little
tease?* His breath all salt and vinegar.

I nodded and gingerly led him home
by the path that winds through the cemetery.

# TRAINEE PRIEST AT ROCHUSKAPELLE

Saint Sebastian stands covered with the hunger-cloth –
a hooded detainee from off the seminary television.
We must give up the sight of him to focus on the bare Easter altar.

Good Friday I will lift the veil, search his face for a clue of agony.
I don't believe the sculptor's lie, he cannot be at peace.
He is like me, young when he gave himself to God.

While the priests are diluting wine
I would have him tug off his sack, step down, walk.
I will lie him across my lap, pull out the cock-feathered arrows,

wash the holes in his body, sew them up
with my mother's darning needle, ask if I will be forgiven
for wanting his delicate blood on my fingers.

But Sebastian is carved, I have traced the chisel's evidence
with my thumb. I know my thread can't heal –
he and his arrows are of the same body of Milanese oak.

There is no stop where either wound or weapon begin –
our devotion is a perpetual hurt. I am like him,
young, bound for a lifetime of suffering behind cloth.

# SANDCASTLES

A tall gent waits
inside the playground
not looking at anyone

but rather mostly
at the dog-dark door
of the public lavs

and the shadows
pooling within.

I wish I could enjoy
forging sandcastles with you
and your two year old,

filling the lime-green bucket,
packing it down
with the luminous shovel . . .

only now this man is
watching me –

he's caught me
amongst the families,
caught me trying to play daddy.

His gaze is iron-heavy
as he walks
to the lavatory door,

pauses, like he were crossing a road,
then enters.

In one version of the poem I
follow him in, slide up next to the cistern.
He bolts the grimy cubicle door
behind us. Unzips my jeans.

In another I stay building with your daughter,
perfecting the castle's keep, the last place to be breached
in a siege. In another I'm disgusted by these queers
who hang around toilets trying to catch my eye.

In another I am your husband – I yearn to leave
our daughter alone for just a handful of minutes –
she'd be fine out here – knowing there is more love
for me in there, with him.

In the last version I am your daughter,
sculpting the intricate castle from damp sand
pitted through with fag ends and gum –
oblivious to the men, the poem being written.

# REPORTAGE

When I read how they poured petrol over that man
I see my own death in some minor fictitious Baltic state.
Men I went to school with drag me into the arable scrub
chanting *queer!* in a different language – they slip off
my hood, wet my body with tractor fuel; the ringleader
spits in my face before pulling out his tarnished Zippo –
eyes skittering with white hate, his hand steady
and as if Europe were a funfair mirror I look back
across the thousand miles of moving corn, the brick-wall
estates, the shuttered-up villages – to see myself free,
pacing the avenues of a liberal city, scanning a tabloid –
poem forming in my head. We are not so different
that poor sod and I – I too was born into this world to have
dirt on my knees, another man's saliva in my mouth.

# BEHEADING OF A FEMALE SAINT

*After Gherardo di Jacopo Starnina*


I have come to the gallery
to witness the execution
of a woman

her golden underskirt
moves
in the wind outside the airless city

they hold sticks to lance
the headless corpse
each man wears a hat

Olybrius
Governor of Antioch
are you among them?

you would have placed your arms
around her neck
lain down with her

the grey stone
has let through
very few flowers this year

the river runs gold
the blank sky
is gold

women watch
from within
the red town

none anticipate
the silence
that will follow

look
even as the black sword
is above her head

Margaret's hands
are still cupped
in prayer

## COVER-BOYS

top shelf rags are not always pink curves&tits
sometimes an out of date *LATIN INCHES* hides
forgotten behind *RAZZLE* – three pixelated pricks
have stayed this hard since two-thousand and five –
José Raúl Hotrod have stood inked jaw-locked
in a three-way french for some nine rugged years –
pecs still greasy tans Miami-orange fingers tucked
into each other's pits – interests include *PS3* beer
skateboarding fisting being taken for expensive meals –
this is the future I wish for them – open-mouthed
wanton lithe&toned – instead of the all too real –
Wikipedia tells me Hotrod married a girl appalled
by his past – Raúl's serving time for battery in Bristol
Texas a born-again homophobe&José's heart exploded
on stage at Pride too much love or rather crystal

# MY STAG

Ian Taverner, for a 50p bet,
peeled and jointed a stag beetle
with his red penknife –
ripping off all eight agate legs,
ferreting out the fold-up tiffany lamp wings,
beheading the stag
with a butcher's confidence.

When the dead beetle was laid out,
like a disassembled carburettor,
winking blue-black
in the schoolyard sun,
to complete the bet
Ian chased each body part down
with a swig of cherry cola.

Our gang left grossed out,
but I had the stomach for it, I was in love.
I wiped his pink mouth
with my aertex sleeve,
proudly gripped his surgeon's hand
beneath the battered lunch bench
desperate for his kiss.

# LE JARDIN SECRET

boys were my saplings
my whiff of green my sprouts
a hundred soft palms
reaching for my warmth
boys were my herbs
square-stemmed furred
scented with musk dank clove
& lovage boys were my
crops my ripe-red-yield
my seeds each one exploding
onto my lips like sherbet
boys were my vines my
creepers my climbers
tattooing my neck back
& thighs with suckle boys
were my nettles my thistles
my thorns tickling me with
scratches & painting me
scarlet boys were my berries
my doll's eyes my yew
bitter on the tongue dizzying
& psychedelic boys were my
pitchers my fly-traps my
venus a petaled mouth wet
throat around a grave

## UNDER THE APPLE TREE

Seeing the shirtless red-haired boy
by the shed, like a watchman's shed, I ask for the way

he's much older and I'm a great liar
I've been here before

but this is my first time

in the scrub he pushes me
to my knees then places his fingers in my mouth

as apple blossom, just lighter than skin, brushes his shoulder

but then he says he's got a condom – could fuck me here
if I fancy.

From inside the empty shed I sense
my mother, welling up, as she watches

but I don't stop till he finishes in my mouth.

# JEANNE BARÉ OBSERVES THE INLET

Roosting starlings watch the river continue
its labour. Anglers draw their boats up

onto the sand, erasing the hoof prints of cattle
who retreat into the violet cedars.

And as if they know they are alone ˙
perch rise up out of the dark,

wake the inlet and drive the water mad
grasping for damselfly, beetles, boatmen,

mosquitoes, hawk moth and paper wasp.
This water sport soundtracks the dusk –

inestimable leaps into that other world
through the fearsome belt of oxygen.

All of us are capable of great change;
you only have to watch the fish transform

into dark birds swooping the surface at enormous speed
to know.

# MAZ

In the barbershop beneath my building
the boys are listening to Bengali rap.
A bearded one, perhaps nineteen, sharpens a cutthroat razor
upon an ancient leather belt
crisscrossed with cuts like a butcher's block
when a young man enters.

They shake hands, pull in for a half hug
then a towel is offered, tucked in around his athletics sweater.
The boy gestures to the smiling porcelain sink,
his thick forearm toned from the blade's repeated action,
then gently tilts his customer's head
against warm running water –
glittering like scales
caked on a fishmonger's palms.
He begins to lather. Suds run down the customer's muscular neck
and over the loops of his gang tattoo,
fingers slide in and out of wet soaped hair.

I can almost see my face
in the glistening black crew-cut.
I have stopped outside the shop window
in the otherwise empty street to watch.
The boy's eyes catch mine, he does not look away.
He knows why I am watching.

# MATINS

After singing at church he walks the mile to the bathhouse
and enters the fug of men.
Not the smaller cabins intended for twos and threes
but the steam room
for the hands, the lips
that emerge from interior clouds
to work him in warm silence, kissing the head, anointing the shaft

as he recalls the altar's lavish cloth
pouring down onto the cool stone floor,
the polished, perhaps solid-gold, candlesticks holding their burdens of white
slow-burning wax
and the kneeling figures in their scarlet robes
washing the grey taken-down body.
A woman has placed her fingers into the red hinge of a chest wound.
Below the words read:

*Save me O God for the waters are come in*
*even unto my soul.*

# PERMISSIONS

I am always writing my pamphlet of abuse poems          collecting rapey verse
like a tramp pocketing bin-butts      fuse 'em together later          have one mag-
nificent slow cigarette          when my chap is read readers will          sharp
intake of breath          just as they do          mid-poetry-slam over a glass of house

red      white      pink whatever tickles your          how daring how dark what
marvellous images          the one about what was it the          schoolboy's sphincter
being like a          I never realised how pink          the inside          of a cheek
confessional          surely not this writer wasn't          that would be too awful

but how does one ask outright          my dear boy          is the I you well
I am not hinting anymore          please take your hand out of my trousers

# FISHMONGER

Every Thursday he came to call
in his blood-licked surgeon's coat
and if my sister was out
I knew to order nothing but eggs
as his prices for fish were far too dear.

Once he took me into his van –
row upon row of gleaming flanks,
the rough brick-armour of crabs,
the stopped hearts of bivalves pickled in brine,
all resting on clouds of ice.

He let me dowse his catch in ammonia
*a secret to keep their sparkle*, he said
and as I sprayed they spluttered
back to life – mouths gurning for water,
gills rippling like Venetian blinds,

coppers and silvers flashing and lathering.
I heard the mighty roar of the sea
surround his van like traffic.
He took me into his capable arms
and I did not cry out.

He fed me prawns, wiped
the brine from my lips –
let me try my first razor clam
unzipped from its pale hard shell
the tip, soft and white and saline.

In that battered old Transit
I took the whole ocean into my mouth
and then he sent me home
with a dozen eggs –
church-cold, freckled, unbroken.

## ADMISSION
*for E. D.*


Ed asks if my poems are authentic
do I have any experience in the matter
and by this he means abuse
and by this he means have I been a victim
I tell him the truth he talks to cover my silence
the Nigerian playwright who writes only
of the Second Liberian Civil War
how trauma is a shared thread
leading to other victims of molestation
how rape is a weapon blame

still in truth I wish he hadn't asked see I
want this man my friend to see me
as pure not in any way ruined or touched
dirty a tease a liar an attention seeker
he cites Wordsworth something familiar
about tranquillity and I want to ask
now that you know do you still like me
but like the boy when asked by his therapist
to say into the bathroom mirror
it's not your fault I remain dumb

# THE BUTCHER'S APPRENTICE

Above the blue-bottles and dying wasps
I watch his teenage hands
grappling with quartered flesh –
the blonde hairs striped with blood.

He is how I imagine a Grecian statue painted –
poppy-cheeked, sun-burnt skin, eyes white with labour

then comes his mythical paring knife
mottled from use, nicks from when the fine edge
had caught on bone,
handle rubbed away to nothing

and on his salty forehead – blood smear
from the Minotaur's own pelt?

I have imagined myself his victim nightly –
reduced myself to meat
– shin, heart, topside, marrow –
convinced I'll feel nothing as he

cleaves my ribcage in two – my blood rinsing his hands
like the black Mediterranean.

Jealous of the ox, the pig, the calf
I feel my fists split and cloven,
my tongue grows fat – engorged with blood –
the horn buds ferret beneath my forehead –

Oh to be your prey!
Hang me up butcher – my nape is ripe for your hook!

## PILGRIMAGE
*for S. T. F.*


How you loved Jesus –
found him everywhere
even the rank queer bars of Vauxhall.

You would lead his drug-scorched body to a cubicle,
lift his stone-white vest,
kiss his side

injured with the tattooed names of boys
and once
a skin-coloured dove

carrying a twig in its skin-coloured beak –
searching for land
across a sun-tanned midriff.

## DANCING BEAR

Children bring me coins
to watch him balançoire, tombé –
they imagine he has a
forest inside, they close
their eyes to see him
foraging on a high cliff
above a burnished lake –
belly to the wet earth
but inside is just a savage
who loves with only his
claws, his wild mouth,
tears at honeyed flesh
with his barbed tongue
so I tamed him with
a rod, a crop, my fist –
starved him until he would
dance this way, that way.
At six o'clock you should
see me count my money –
hatfuls of brass and gold.
I uncouple his snout, rub
a drop of lotion in, pour
myself a drink as my
father unzips his bear skin –
places his naked head
on my lap – throat exposed.
He apologises to me
for all the places on my body
his hands have scarred
but I just close his eyes,
sing him to sleep,
nuzzle his ears – a blade
in my other hand.

# WOUND

In the car home I ask if my foreskin's
been kept by the surgeon –
pickled perhaps in a specimen jar.
You say he has almost certainly burnt it.

We are bringing home a cream
dangerous as glass, to apply
on my new skin – just
above the *cavernous branch*

but I stall before the bath
intended to soften the wound
so your hand
takes over.
          I guess you really loved me,
pulling back, revealing something like
what hides in a shell – soft,
unused to air.

Your palm sticks
to my gluey cut. I cry out
but you slap my thigh, afraid I won't heal
if the cream isn't applied.

And I'm terrified my dick will tear,
the tiny black stitches like bugs
bedding down for a feed on my prick
and it stinks.

For months I forewent rubbing – that
not-quite-named-yet private pleasure,
afraid I would rip, worried
the surgeon had named a fault line,
always at risk, ready to split.

But eventually I had to,
so I thought of the surgeon, his kind face,
his moustache. How he touched me
with his fingers, then his sterilized equipment
and then you, daddy, lotioning my scab.

The wound stung as I tugged.

# TEST

*That's my son's birthday*
and before she can readjust her face
I catch pity.

I am being asked the inevitable questions:
age, how many lovers, were they from the EU –
things I tell her, more or less.

She boozes up my elbow bend,
unpeels a fresh bright needle.
I look away to see

the wall with its proud bubble writing
RAINBOW WARRIORS FACING IT TOGETHER
and a pamphlet advertising chastity.

*We were careful though*
I offer as an apology.
Her syringe begrudgingly fills, splutters,

she draws out leaving a bead of guilty blood
on the crook of my arm.
*You'll know in three hours darling, for better or worse.*

# PUBLIC TOILETS IN REGENT'S PARK

The men here are bird-footed
feathering past the attendant's two-way mirror
unperturbed by the colonizing micro-organisms –
*bulleidia    cobetia    shigellosis*

sliming across the yellowed groutings,
the fist-deep pool of brackish water
quivering in the U-bend, the tile that reads
*for information on venereal disease telephone 01 . . .*

All for the thrill of placing their knees
on the piss stained cold, the iris shimmering
behind a hand-carved glory hole,
a beautiful cock unfolding like a swan's neck
from the Harris Tweed of a city gent's suit.

Whispers, gasps of contact echo
inside each nested cubicle! But careful –
the prying attendant will rattle
her bucket and mop if she spies four shoes!
Our men disperse as mallards from the face of a pond.